AWARE Traders! BEWARE

ABOUT THE AUTHOR

When working in a newspaper 10 years ago, I used to invest in blue-chip companies or medium-scale, fundamentally strong companies and booked reasonable profits. Sometimes, I was involved in trading as well. Then, I worked as a senior dealer in various stock broking concerns where I dealt with clients. i.e punched orders whenever clients wanted to do Buying and selling of securities, Future & options contracts, etc., for clients and I was keeping abreast of stock market-related news, Analysis, Global and Domestic Economic Indicators to update them for facilitating to do trading or making invest, and now, I am working in the customer care department in a stock broking concern. Hence, I think I can share some of my experience with you as an investor, trader, and dealer.

S. No	Table of Contents	Page No
1.	Basic Knowledge of the share market (Stock market)	4
2.	Futures & Options Trading	
	(i) Future Trading	10
	(ii) Hedging	15
	(iii) Options Trading	17
3	Conclusion	21

Basic Knowledge of the share market (Stock market)

In this article, no act in our law, internal details, etc have been employed for simple understanding.

You may cross various petty shops, tea shops, small hotels, etc., while walking over streets or riding bicycles, etc. These tiny establishments are mainly owned and controlled by individual persons. For instance, Sukumar is the owner of Ramaswamy's petty shop. That is, he is the only person who invested the money to run this petty shop. Nobody except him can enjoy the profit made out of running this shop. However, he will be the only sufferer when his shop makes any losses. This individual ownership is known as a sole proprietorship.

There are also various other shops or business establishments that are managed, controlled, and owned by two or more persons. These business units are known as partnership firms. In these types of business units, profits or losses are shared among two or more persons equally or based on the profit-sharing ratio as per the agreement made between them. These persons are called partners. Here, you can notice the word "Share" emerged in these types of businesses.

All these partners share (make) their contribution (investments) to run a partnership firm. Hence, all partners share their ownership rights equally or based on their agreement.

Now, I think you understand the meaning of "share" a little bit.

So, I desire to come to the main part:- Now, you know about sole proprietorship and partnership firms.

Usually, in partnership, friends, and relatives come and join together to commence and run a new business to share the profit.

Then, the concept of the company comes to the fore. It is a large type of business where a huge amount of money is required.

A person, who has only a capital of Rs. 50 crores, can begin a new business with an investment of Rs. 100 crores, as he has various options to raise the remaining Rs. 50 crores. One option to raise remaining funds is sharing his ownership with the public. That is, he will invite the public to buy (subscribe) his shares (of the company) through the method of public issues (initial public offer method). In this method, he will invite the public by issuing a prospectus in which people can find highlights and risk factors of his company, the maximum and minimum number of shares required to be applied, etc. After going through the prospectus, if the public is satisfied with the business, they will apply for shares through applications issued by him by paying the cost of shares announced in newspapers, TV, etc. The person who desires to commence business is called the founder or the promoter of the company.

Sometimes, some public issues are over-subscribed by the public. In that situation, shares will be allotted on a pro-rata basis. That is, if we consider the above example since the promoter has Rs.50 crores, he needs to collect only Rs. 50 crores additionally. Suppose the public applied shares for more than the ownership he decides to share, he will allot those shares on a pro-rata basis. That is, for Rs. 50 crores, if he gets Rs. 75 crores, he will return Rs. 25 crores to the public itself who has applied. For instance, if a person applied for 100 shares in this public issue, he will get only 75 shares and the remaining amount for 25 shares will be refunded to him.

As above mentioned things happen in the initial stages, this is known as the primary market.

If an investor gets an allotment for 100 shares, after some time if he wants to convert his shares into money, he has to go to a market called the secondary market. There, he sells his shares and gets his money. Naturally, investors will sell their shares only when the value of their shares gets increased in the market (secondary market).

In India, the main marketplaces are the National Stock Exchange (NSE) and the Bombay Stock Exchange (BSE) where investors can buy and sell shares through recognized share brokers who are members of these stock exchanges.

Futures & Options Trading

Future Trading:-

Actually, the contracts are traded in futures and options markets, unlike stocks in the equity market. These contracts derive their value from the underlying assets i.e., the stock future contracts and stock options derive their values from their respective underlying stocks like Reliance, Infosys, etc., whereas the Index futures and Index options get their value from their respective Indices like Nifty, Bank Nifty, etc.,. The futures and options contracts are too traded in the Currency segment as well. In equity, the market lot size denotes a (one) quantity of the stock. However, in Futures & Options Trading, a lot size represents the quantities of underlying instruments in large quantities.

I am furnishing below the present lot sizes of NSE for some of the Indices and stock contracts in which numbers appear in the column of the monthly contracts of 23-

Apr, 23-May, 23-Jun, etc., indicate quantities of a lot of sizes of respective Indices and stock contracts for understanding:-

UNDERLYING	SYMBOL	23-Apr	23-May	23-Jun	23-Sep	23-Dec	24-Mar	24-Jun	24-Dec	25-Jun	25-Dec
NIFTY FINANCIAL SERVICES	FINNIFTY	40	40	40							
NIFTY MID SELECT	MIDCPNIFTY	75	75	75							
NIFTY BANK	BANKNIFTY	25	25	25	25	25	25				
NIFTY 50	NIFTY	50	50	50	50	50	50	50	50	50	50
Derivatives on Individual Securities	Symbol	23-Apr	23-May	23-Jun							
AARTI INDUSTRIES LTD	AARTIIND	850	850	850							
ABB INDIA LIMITED	ABB	250	250	250							
ALKEM LABORATORIES LTD.	ALKEM	200	200	200							
ABBOTT INDIA LIMITED	ABBOTINDIA	40	40	40							
ASIAN PAINTS LIMITED	ASIANPAINT	200	200	200							
BHEL	BHEL	10500	10500	10500							
CANARA BANK	CANBK	2700	2700	2700							
GAIL (INDIA) LTD	GAIL	9150	9150	9150							
ACC LIMITED	ACC	250	250	250							
HDFC LTD	HDFC	300	300	300							
HDFC BANK LTD	HDFCBANK	550	550	550							
ADITYA BIRLA CAPITAL LTD.	ABCAPITAL	5400	5400	5400							
HERO MOTOCORP LIMITED	HEROMOTOCO	300	300	300							
HINDALCO INDUSTRIES LTD	HINDALCO	1400	1400	1400							
APOLLO HOSPITALS ENTER. L	APOLLOHOSP	125	125	125							
HINDUSTAN PETROLEUM CORP	HINDPETRO	2700	2700	2700							
HINDUSTAN UNILEVER LTD.	HINDUNILVR	300	300	300							

Even though the margin requirements for doing intraday trades came into existence in the equity segment too under SEBI's new regulation mechanism like future contracts and selling of the options contracts, though the trading occurs in market lots in both segments, a market lot size is just a quantity for all scrips in equity segment whereas the market lot size differs for scrips, traded in the future contracts and selling options contracts as shown in above present lot size details of NSE which are comparatively larger than as that of for market lot sizes of equity segment. Hence, the intraday and carry-forward trading in the future contracts and selling of the options contracts is highly riskier than intraday trading in the equity segment.

Hedging:-

Actually, these contracts came into existence for hedging purposes in the past. Believe, a farmer begins to propagate paddy tomorrow, He can reap the benefit of this only after three or four months. He doesn't know at which rate he can sell his produce after three or four months. He is likely to earn profit or lose his money. He will make a selling contract with a buyer for his produce at a future date for a profit to save him from loss.

Likewise, the export companies will sell the Us dollar against Rupees whenever the currency markets go downwards in the value of the Us dollar against Rupees and the import companies will do conversely when there is a hawkish trend in their remitted currency value against ours.

This process is known as Hedging. The hedging technique will likely minimize the loss only. There is very less chance of making any profits in Hedging. Indeed, Hedging provides protection or insurance to the buying or selling positions.

Similarly, the traders/merchants do hedging at the time of the diminishing of their stock value by selling their same stock's one month, two months, three months, etc., stock contracts in the future markets to minimize their shortfall. Equally, they do the same thing in their future contracts too. i.e., when the trader sold near month contract when the market goes towards the northward direction, they can buy for the same far month contract against their selling positions.

Options Trading:-

Despite this, Options trading too does come under the future segment. It differs from futures trading. There are two types of options. One is a call option and the other is a put option. The buyer of both the call and put option contracts has the right to buy the underlying assets before expiration or at the maturity of the contracts but does not have obligation to do it. The buyer has the risk only to the extent of the premium bought by them when the Index or stock options go against his position. However, the seller or the writer of the call/put options has only the obligation to buy or sell by paying only the margin amount as determined by exchanges as like that of the future contracts, they are having the same risk as the traders who are participating in the speculative trading of futures market which includes intraday and carry forward positions.

However, the seller or the writer of the call/put options has only the obligation to buy or sell by paying only the margin amount as determined by exchanges as like that of the future contracts, they are having the same risk as the traders who are participating in the speculative trading of futures market which includes intraday and carry forward positions.

As each option contract has time value, though there are movements of the prices in the corresponding stocks/Indices in the equity segment, the buyer of the options too has the risk of losing their money, when they carry forward their positions i.e., the buying value (premium) of the option will get decreased when each day of the contract is nearing its expiry date. This especially happens to most of the "out of the money" and at contracts and occurs even to many "in the money" contracts.

The exchange fixes 5 strike prices over the spot prices and 5 of them below it, and one at like to the spot price for the call and put options in a month.

When the strike prices of the call options which exceed above spot prices are known as "Out the money" options, the strike prices which are all below spot prices are known as "In the money" options and those strike prices are equivalent to spot prices will be called as "At the money option". The trader/merchant will get a profit when he exercises the "In the money" option, he will incur a loss at exercising the "out the money option and arrive at a breakeven point when he exercises the "At the money option".

The traders/merchants can utilize hedging techniques in options trading too.

For instance,

When the trader/ merchant buys a contract of Nifty future, He needs to buy nifty in the options market to hedge against his Nifty future position. Then he can minimize his loss when the market moves against his bought position in the Nifty future.

Conclusion:-

Hence, there is a little bit of a general perception in the minds of some of our people that the stock market means speculation. Others, too, go with them to some extent, as speculation is highly happening in the stock market. However, the stock market should not be included under the term "speculation" alone. The good investors, not engaging themselves in speculation activity, make investments in the blue chip companies after weighing the fundamental aspects of these companies and furthermore, they have adequate endurance to stay over a longer period of days to reap the benefits of investments. I mentioned in my previous E-book titled "A GUIDE TO STOCK MARKET TRADING:- Real Facts About Stock Markets" that disciplined trading will not put anybody into great trouble. Hence, they do not get trapped in greediness when the traders get involved in intraday trading activities in the equity segment, speculative trading in the future, and options segment, etc., which will drag them to a greater loss.

There is one more cause that remains in this market which is the sentimental factor. This aspect has great dominance over the market comparing other analyses. The market fluctuates mainly on the sentimental efforts of the country's economy, including variations in government policies, climatic conditions, wars, bomb blasts, etc. However, nobody can have control over these types of features.

A similar type of factor is also especially applicable to carry forward positions in the F&O segment. When any sentimental factors occur the traders can have control over their positions and come out of their positions with limited loss in intraday trading either in F&O trading or in equity trading, when any adverse things occur politically, economically, etc., globally as well as domestically. However, when they carry forward their positions, the same unexpected incidents happen overnight, and the adverse impact of carrying forward their positions will be greater. Besides, it is also better to close positions Intraday itself, when any major announcements identical to the changes in monetary policies of central banks like the decisions of the US Federal Reserve, Reserve Bank of India, etc., regarding monetary policies are expected the next day and when there are market shutdowns for two or more days.

Complete support is not given for fundamental analysis by outlining the above-mentioned details. There are too some risk factors involved i.e., the companies may possess strong fundamentals during the time of going by the records of these companies. These performances may not be sustained in the future due to various sentimental, macro, or microeconomic factors. However, greater chances of success are possible, if everyone stays as an investor and makes investments in the highly reputed concerns. Hence, investors are advised to keep a close watch on news concerning companies, and the economy so as well to succeed in their endeavor to obtain satisfactory benefits for their investments. Before making any investment decisions, they should carefully read the necessary documents and follow authenticated information concerning particular companies/companies or particular investments.